Cat's Painting

Jan Burchett and Sara Vogler ● Jonatronix

OXFORD
UNIVERSITY PRESS

In this story ...

Cat

Nok

Miss Jones

Cat was painting. She had just painted a tree.

"Can I help to finish it?" Nok said,
jumping from the pot.

"You might spoil it," said Cat.
"No, I will not!" he said.

Nok pointed at the paintbrush. Power
shot from his hands.

The brush stood up! It started to zig-zag across the painting.

"Stop it, Nok," said Cat, grabbing the brush.

Nok went to the red paint.
Cat shrank and ran after him.

Nok ran across the painting. He left a trail of footprints.

Then Nok slid in the wet paint.

He hit the paint pots and they fell.

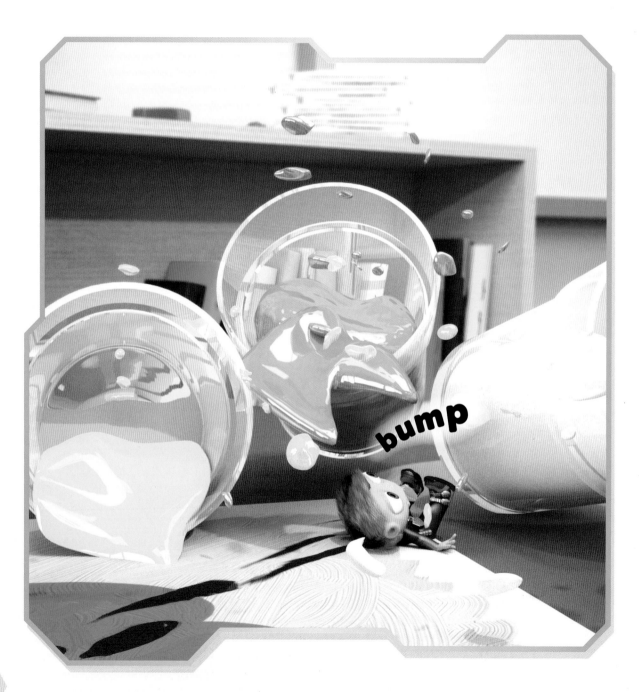

"Look at this mess," Cat said. "I need to clear up."
Nok felt bad.

"Look at this painting," said Miss Jones. "It's so good."

"See," said Nok, with a grin.
"I did help!"

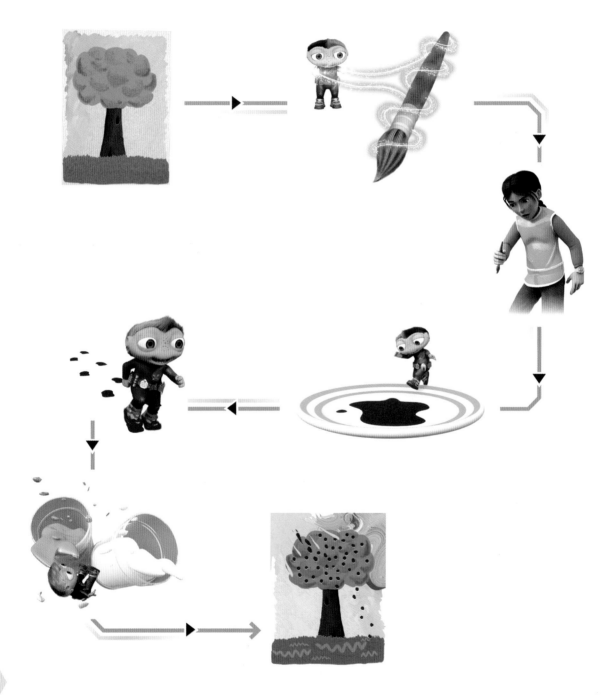